How to become a Talented Manager?

By
Chakrapani Srinivasa

How to Become a Talented Manager?

By

Chakrapani Srinivasa

About the Author

Chakrapani Srinivasa (Padmaja), Freelance journalist from India possesses Bachelor degree in Engineering (B.E) and Post graduate in Business Management (MBA) with Distinction. He has worked as Associate Editor of 'Naradar' fortnightly journal in Chennai, India. He is the Senior Editor of the journal "The Divineness".

Contributed articles, short stories and travelogues in leading journals like Ananda Vikatan, Kumudam, Savi, Kalki, Dinamani Kadhir, Dinamani daily, Idhayam Pesukirathu, Naradar etc

He has written articles and e books through Smashwords Inc, Kindle Direct Publishing, Atlanta Publications, Cooperjal Publications (UK), lulu.com, ezinearticles.com, shvoong.com, iproclaim.com (USA) and News Agency in (Germany).

He is the Consulting Editor of Contemporary Who's Who-Research Board of Advisers of ABI, USA.

View his other books :
https://www.amazon.com/s?k=chakrapani+srinivasa&i=digital-text&page=2&qid=1595769939&ref=sr_pg_2

Preface

To become a talented and good Professional Manager, you should first know about the basics of Professional Management.

The capability of an individual to manage money, men, materials and machines with rich experience in hand in that field can be pin pointed as Professional Management.

This style of functioning needs no educational harvest in Harvard School of management or in any business schools.   Whatever he sees, whatever he does, whatever he imagines, whatever he speculates and whatever he manipulates everything arises out of the foundation – the practical experience. He never goes after a book for his actions executed. Peter. F. Druckers is not his God Father for his style of function.

A unique skill in a particular field enabled him to master and monitor all aspects of smooth running of an organization. His only aim is to make the company always sail in a safe boat. The guidance for his vision is nothing but the company's objectives. He meticulously follows it with all vigor and puts forth his abundant experience into action.

Contents

Professional Management

To become a talented and good Professional Manager you should first know about the basics of Professional Management!

The capability of an individual to manage money, men, materials and machines with rich experience in hand in that field can be pin pointed as Professional Management.

This style of functioning needs no educational harvest in Harvard School of management or in any business schools. Whatever he sees, whatever he does, whatever he imagines, whatever he speculates and whatever he manipulates everything arises out of the foundation – the practical experience. He never goes after a book for his actions executed. Peter. F. Druckers is not his God Father for his style of function.

A unique skill in a particular field enables him to master and monitor all aspects of smooth running of an organization. His only aim is to make the company always sail in a safe boat. The guidance for his vision is nothing but, the company's objectives. He meticulously follows it with all vigor and puts forth his abundant experience into action.

To gain the classic art of Professional Management one has to reinforce his duration in that field with brimful of various experiences. Without this vast experience he cannot turn out to be an efficient Professional Management student.

But for an individual, who has a basic study on Management in any recognized Business Management Institution, he is bound to be more successful manager or administrator in the organization at the outset itself. All the positive and negative sides of the administration are spoon fed to him in his study course and he is enlightened in the administration field right from the early years of his profession. He is like a 'Ready Made Shirt' rather than going for a cloth, then go after a tailor etc. When he enters an organization, he has a pre-occupied brain with management techniques.

A professional management will flower well only after a long period of an individual's existence in that company. This is a time consuming phenomena to gain skill to administrate. Some actions may be misleading and one has to learn only by mistakes he has committed due to this Professional Management. But a person qualified in the Art of Management will have a better vision in this execution of power and extraction of work.

"As far as I am concerned, Professional Management is a gift fetched out of sheer experience" says a leading industrialist.

The management of the organization M/s Neyveli Lignite Corporation rightly fits into the criterion of Professional Management only. Hence a case study is presented at the end of this book.

Right from the present Chairman to a worker in the field, all employees are imbibed due to Professional

Management. He is only a Mining Man with abundant skill in mining, both metal and underground mining. Out of the experience in different mines, he has gained a strong ground in the organization – as the leader of 20000 employees. What he practiced was truly a symbol of Professional Management. So, also did the Ex-Chairman of that organization. Everyone follows suit.

'So the King so his men' is the old saying. All the employees have earned technical know-how and acclimatized to the attitude of the workmen they move with. With these talents in hand they have mastered the skill in Professional Management.

The management gives importance to experience, which enables the individual to manage men, machines and funds of the organization. Hence that organization safely and rightly fits for the study on Professional Management.

To Promote Professionalism

All careful steps are to be taken to promote professionalism to achieve the expected results and fulfill the hunger for profit.

Your organization's aims, destination and objectives should be borne in mind for placing the first step in this study of Professional Management.

An aimless movement will negate the success.

At the outset the manager should be alert to watch and see that all activities are sailing towards the right desired directions set by the top management. No deviation should be tolerated as it will result in distortion of the progress picture.

Your organization's aim may be to attain continuous production to reach the target to get the desired profitable revenue. Hence this aim should be forced into everyone's mind and action to achieve our main objective.

So, if any action or manipulation does not fetch the desired production, then instructions should be given by that manager to set right it without hesitation.

Since full production is the criteria, signboards indicating the importance of production, which gives revenue for the organization, should be displayed.

For example:
'Power is money'.
'Loss of generation is loss of your future'!

Also safety should go hand in hand with production. That should be the criteria of the organization. Hence it is to be seen that safety slogans are displayed in all vulnerable points in the field. Safety slogan competition can be arranged for the workmen and staff to make them realize what the organization aims at. Prizes can be given to the best slogans. Also dramas can be conducted to enforce safety in the plant.

Growth and Competition:
Healthy competition should always exist for good growth of the organization. To compete with other

competing organization all efforts should be taken to single out the right machinery, men and financial resources to build the immaculate image of the organization.

It is always wise to insist to select the circuits and equipments designed by an internationally reputed company in the electrical and electronic field to see that a high standard of return in quality is obtained and trouble free running of the unit is maintained for full production. Also leading consultants like Tata Consultancy Services should be engaged for sorting out all production problems and see the required target is achieved.

It is also good to ask them to go for spare parts and auxiliary equipments supplied by reputed concerns so that breakdown is minimized. This will boost the image of the company, amongst other competitors.

Above are the internal factors concerned with the growth of an organization.

Regarding the external influence like Government support, it is good to raise funds by floating shares since your company has to depend on its own resources.

Profit is the Ultimate Requirement

You should ensure that the percentage of profit gained every year exceeds the previous year.

The production costs should be calculated and also the selling price of product will be enhanced correspondingly. This should be driven home in everybody's mind. This sort of execution will consider the welfare of the organization as a whole. All wastages should be curbed to see that profit is steered in the right direction. Steps are to be taken to reduce the wastages to see that loss is minimized.

Research and Development:

Full efforts are to be taken for research and development program for improvement in production. Quality is the key word for success in an organization. Hence give importance for any modification in electrical circuits, mechanical application and operational activities. The motive behind it is to have wider knowledge and scope for innovation, which will enable to compete with other organizations.

While screening the applications for selecting personnel for a job, see that merit is given top priority and recommendations are rejected totally. The efficiency of an individual very much affects the path leading to the success of an organization.

We should maintain a team spirit in the industry to have a smooth understanding between operation and maintenance staff so that a perfect coordination exists to achieve full target.

Congenial Atmosphere and Job Satisfaction

To have talented men under us alone is one part of the success story and the efforts taken to retain them in our organization is the other part of the overall success of the organization.

Once selection is over give a lively atmosphere for them to work and see no interference spoils their mood to work. Abundant freedom, at the same time expect them to give the desired results is an art of extracting work from the personnel with excellence.

Allocation of jobs as per their desire and providing extra nourishing and smoothening atmosphere to induce them to put in all their talents and efforts will work out well.

A moral support for the genuine intelligent and inspiring workers is a 'must' for a growing concern.

Telling words of appreciation and praise right in front of his face will do wonders. Every individual will hanker for encouragement and it will be first and foremost duty to see that the creative ideas of all the deserving persons are boosted to the maximum extent.

This will accelerate his loyalty to the organization and urge him to serve better for reaching the all time success for the concern. He will be in an exalted mood and start doing his work without waiting for anybody's instructions.

Effective Leadership:

A salient feature of success is good leadership. An excellent lead given by a Chairman will definitely lead the company to glorious success. Give due recognition to good leadership talents and see the individuals feel their esteem self at all times.

As a leader give a helping hand to all the needs of your subordinates and lend your ear to their grievances round the clock without any reservation and hesitation. Their rapport is a must for a growing concern and good professional management.

Reward the talents of your subordinates and encourage them to work more and build their confidence. Always set an exemplary attitude and careful step in all spheres and promote that discipline amongst your subordinates.

A well planned decisions and good vision should be encouraged and mooted by you to your fellow men and enable them to carry on the goods to reach the desired goal.

Transformation of Creativity for Flourishing Business

Giving new ideas regarding to work is a matter to be patted at the back. But will the implementation of this idea fetch results?

This aspect should be monitored with utmost care and dexterity. Then only a complete figure of prosperity and success can be achieved.

Hence see that you implement this aspect positively. Give freedom of thought, freedom speech and action but insist that the work is completed with the anticipated perfection.

Tell them that you need full production in your plant and they may take any measures, alterations and adjustments even if it deviates from the normal routine procedures.

For example in a factory a technician in a division may not turn up for duty. In case of emergency it will be wise to permit a technician from another division, who is talented and experienced to see that the production is maintained. You can compensate for his additional responsibility by granting a C.off for a day, which he can avail on any convenient day.

Also if a modification is suggested by an electrical staff in a circuit, freely ask him to do it and see that modification positively gives a trouble free operation of circuit breakers to enable us to get the full production.

It may be in Civil, Mechanical, Electronics and Telecommunications; any improvement can be welcomed by you without any prejudice. Allow them to implement it and get the desired output with cost and time consciousness.

A new item introduced can be published in your company's home magazine, which will please not only the individual but the whole working community. This will boost others too to evolve new methods of operational technologies in the plant, which will achieve our sole aim!

Ideas and outstanding developments made in production field can be represented to New Delhi to consider for an invention award for that individual.

Suggestion Box can be placed at all work spots and recognition like two increments and out of turn promotion can be given to these individuals. A job satisfaction will came out with flying colors in their mind with all good spirit and tempo.

Replenishing Outmoded Ideas and Skills

A sense of boredom often captures experienced hands involving the routine work for a long period. They will have a thirst to do something different from the routine.

A sort of exertion and mental depression may conquer them and they will hanker for a new line of experience.

Knowing this inner desire, enforce all steps to see that job rotation and special training programs within India and abroad can be given at any cost.

Refresher courses, group discussions, in-plant training and workshop new methods can be bestowed upon them.

It can be given to all categories with full liberation of funds for expenditures incurred for it. This is bound to influence their improvement in advanced knowledge in their field and also have a sense of superiority in their work.

'Experience always pays' should be your motto of administration. Your rapport to them should be a full-fledged one.

A new look is a must!

Always prefer a new look.

Even reputed company products like Surf, Rin etc add a word 'New' on their cover of the packet. This will make the customer to go for it with a hope of a change.

Monotonous is always disliked by many. Hence this magic word 'New' finds a place in almost all products, even Horlicks, boasts by saying New Horlicks with extra Calcium, 'New' is a term liked by old and young. A new dress, a new cinema, a new building, a new pen, a new model... so this new aspect can be introduced by you in your administration with tooth and nail.

To meet the routine competition give all support for a change.

Encourage this phenomenon amongst your fellow men. Just hint them a new idea and make them think and analyze and improve their creativity.

If there is a need for a change in a pattern of work in any area, then you can pin point and say that you need a new method, which is a must for better production.

This will make the subordinates to think a lot and put their heads together to give a solution, which will please you and the organization.

'Old wine in a new cup' is the saying which you can adorn in your mind and also go for a new drink with a new splendor taste and mood!!

Carry on Computers

We are in a Computer Century. Each and everything is computerized. Right from Grocery shop A/c to Bank A/c everything is computerized. Children are learning it at the age of 6 in many schools. They are prepared for the challenging trend, which computer has given to the entire world.

If this is the case, you have the full rights to computerize your activities in your organization.

You can encourage your subordinates to learn computer operations, programming and techniques. Though this will reduce man power you can see that the entire manpower are redesigned in various works concerned with computer maintenance, purchase, remodeling of software etc. Hence a sense of improvement awareness will be in-built in them.

You can arrange books on computers in office technical library for ready reference. Computer magazines can be circulated amongst them to enhance their skill in computers.

At present a messenger may physically take messages from one division to another division area. But by introducing LAN (Local Area Net Work) we can deliver the goods in no time with delicacy. WAN (Wide Area Network) can be utilized for passing on information from State to State and other regions.

Why should you go for old, hackneyed way of functioning ideas when bountiful new 4G Techniques have come out abundantly in this magnificent world of development?

Politics is a Plague

Political attacks on large organizations often hamper their growth. The functioning of that organization is always the target. So, your only style of functioning is to see that all activities are done with proper legal order with no deviation. This will eventually lead to a political trouble free business.

Even while dealing with workers, they may belong to a ruling party union and hence any stringent measure taken against will reflect upon the State ruler's action against the organization. 'Dharna' done by the Political leaders and local politicians MLAs and MPs to protest against the management's action against their union fellow men is a common feature now. So, see that these factors do not intercept the image of the organization. Managers at low level should keep away from politics and aggressive mood towards the union people.

Also the way in which the matters regarding the organization are conveyed to the press should be monitored. A widely circulated magazine published a news item tarnishing the image of the top management as well as the unscrupulous attitude of an officer.

The correct information was side lined and totally different viewed matters were published. This should be avoided and good communication should be had with the local press reporters, so that salient news with decorum is published about the management to maintain its prestige amongst the public. Relationship with the Press is a very vital factor since any adverse remarks about the company will tarnish the image overnight.

You should have a very cordial and friendly atmosphere with the people whose 'Pen is mightier than sword'.

The public are the investors and they hold shares. Any damaging report will make him to withdraw their support to the management and this will give rise to a fall in buying trend of that share. Hence the market value of the organization will dwindle gradually, which you should avoid totally.

There may be many unions in your organization belonging to various parties. All these unions have a political VIP behind them. Hence their representations are to be dealt with lot of perception.

Politics is an intolerable phenomenon and has to be tackled in the right spirit always.

Pressure from the public comes when the existence of the company is facing a threat due to fall in production. People, who have invested in Shares and Fixed deposit will definitely exercise their anxiety on the management. Hence you have to face this critical aspect with lot of intelligence and vigilance. Never let down the depositors or share holders and take much care to pay the dividend to them. A management is greatly indebted to the beloved shareholders of the company, who are the financial back bones!

Giving Due Importance to Aspirations

In this world of wide and varied developments in communication, every individual is able to know the happenings around him. We have innumerable magazines, TV channels and Internet facilities and it is a boon period for inter-State and international communication. Hence one is able to know what is happening around him and in other organization.

Have a thorough knowledge about the amenities, working conditions and monetary benefits in similar organizations. We can compare your status with them and fight for a good scale of pay.

Hence knowing the aspirations of various levels of personnel you can induct various measures to fulfill their aspirations. If their aspirations are not fulfilled then their interest to work hard will dwindle.

Also, younger generations have a bubbling blood and their aspirations will be a more aggressive in nature. They will demand for a more modern type of living conditions and working atmosphere. These are to be adhered to with all sincerity.

Some personnel may demand more powers to exercise on their subordinates as it is done in other concerns. You have to definitely cope up with their aspirations and induce them to improve their style of administration.

Relationship with various fields

A business has variety of contacts right from raw products to the customer. In your organization this contact may start from the erection of machinery, contractors, sub-contractors and erectors in the initial stage. All dealings with them should be smooth and friendly so that erection works were carried out effectively and accurately.

Next we have to manage the commissioning agents and consultancy group of personnel, who assist the entire job of commissioning works. A good relationship with them is a must to complete a project successfully.

Then we have to see the relationship with staff of various categories, operation and maintenance.

Maintaining good relationship with the customers, who are the receiving end of our product, is essential. A proper understanding with them will help to maintain the prestige of the company.

Any damage to quality will damage your company's image.

Beware!!

Motivational techniques of an organization - Case study

A beautiful well decorated chariot is ready. How to drive the chariot? How to induce the horses to enable us to have a smooth, safe and wonderful ride?

Motivation is the answer.

To make people work is an art by itself. The desire should be kindled within him and all beneficial deeds should become an involuntary action and make him strive for the overall welfare of the organizational objectives.

In an organization, where 20000 employees are engaged in multi-various activities, the motivational techniques vary in different kinds. They have many projects being executed at various locations effectively and efficiently along with many Schools, Theatres and Temples managed by them.

Regarding money, the ultimate aim of any human being engaged in a work has been meticulously manipulated and distributed amongst the employees.

First point to be considered is the salary. Previously a leading MNC was the leading concern in terms of emoluments. But this organization had taken all steps and fought with the Delhi administrators and equal wage pattern was implemented to motivate the personnel in that organization.

Apart from Basic Pay and DA additional two increments have been sanctioned for adhering to Family Planning Programs. Also free gifts like cycle, tailoring machine, mixies etc are distributed for undergoing that operation.

For those who acquire special, additional qualifications like AMIE, B.E and M.E. two additional increments are granted for encouraging academic knowledge they have gained.

Allowances

Allowances for people working in various sections of the plant was considered and distributed accordingly. People working in tough areas were paid the maximum allowance as they are directly exposed to hazardous dust. This motivated them as they will not work if no additional benefit is accrued out of their risky job. Hence this liberalized payment was adopted. Also the water and canteen facilities were first served to those areas. Amenities like rain coat, protection shoes etc were first disbursed to them. Regarding promotions, top priority will be given to them, to motivate.

Additional benefits will be next considered to less hazardous area workers. So, in this respect the monetary benefits were classified according to the risks they undergo.

People working in mines have the dust allowance, depth allowance, monitoring allowance, conveyance allowance and also free pick up from their homes (for officers) and free pick up for all from the entrance up to the work spot.

Subsidiary food items served to all at a concession rate. For meals they charge Rs. 1, even though that meals cost Rs. 14 for the management. The management pays the balance Rs. 13 on behalf of the workers.

In mines they engage Cranes, Dozers, Dumpers, Rear Loaders, Excavators, Shovels, Spreaders, Re-claimers and several other heavy equipments. Separate allowances were given to these operators, to motivate them.

Since there was an open cast mines, allowances vary according to the depth, in which the workers and executives work.

Also regarding incentives, the people working in Lignite bench will be paid more and totally in the organization, people directly involved in production will be getting more than compared to office staffs. People working in canteen, theatres etc will be paid in different levels.

Since work is carried out in mines round the clock, they give shift allowances to encourage them as well as to monitor their health.

Educational allowances were given and also schools were run by the management to educate at free of cost.

Stitching and Washing allowances were given to workers. Also uniforms are given at free of cost.

Apart from these allowances, abroad training programs were arranged for staffs to gain more knowledge.

If they give lectures in Training Divisions, they were paid special emoluments to motivate their additional work, which was a valuable contribution.

Thermal Stations

Here also they have Reclaimers, Bull dozers and Rear loaders in the Lignite handling sections from where lignite is received from mines and loaded to the boilers through conveyors. So, all mining operators' allowances were also given to this lignite yard to motivate them.

In the bunker area where lignite is stored they have special allowances as Lignite allowances, dust allowances, hazardous allowances etc. As in mines these people enjoy many preferences as compared to other sections of the Thermal Station. It is to motivate them as they face lot of hardships in that environment. Regarding promotion too they enjoy benefits. They undergo the three shifts pattern and hence the shift allowances are paid to them.

Other common allowances for washing and stitching are given to these staff also. Incentive scales are high for them.

Boiler area:

In this area we have bunkers, 15 mt level where conveyors lead the lignite to furnace, mill area, where lignite is powdered, drum area (8 mt level) where boiler drum is situated at the top most portion of the furnace. Corresponding to level of workshops and hazardous conditions the level of allowances, incentives are distributed.

In Turbine Area the areas where enormous sound is emanated ear protecting equipments and special allowances are given.

In Chemical plant chemicals are added to purify the water before allowing it to the boiler. Hence the people working here are given chemical allowance to motivate.

Similarly Welders, Turners and Blue Printer Operators are given special allowance for their nature of work.

Hence in the monetary benefit aspects, the management liberally issues allowances to all categories depending on the seriousness of the working condition to motivate them to work.

This Township is fully created and maintained by the management for the employees to motivate. Loan for building houses, buying vehicles, marriage, education etc are given liberally.

To motivate the education amongst the employees' sons and daughters, special prizes are given by the management for top rankers and scholarships for higher education.

The management encourages sportsmen by giving preference for job and other trainings. If they are engaged in office work, special permissions are granted for practice sessions to motivate their skill. They can go on 'On Duty' to attend various matches.

Special tournaments are organized by the organization to entertain sports loving employees to have a cheerful atmosphere.

A well maintained library having thousands of invaluable books and magazines have been built for the welfare of the public.

A mobile library van has been arranged to visit all points in the Township to enable reading habit in all sectors of the Township. Reading rooms have been installed in various locations to entertain the public by providing all leading Newspapers, Magazines etc.

These are all motivating factors for creating a healthy and well cared atmosphere.

Prayer is a must for mental peace. So, considering this aspect the management has taken all steps to provide Prayers for all religions. Many Temples are maintained by the organization under the control of the Township Administrator. It is all for the welfare of the staffs, who wishes to relax their mind after days toil.

A marriage hall suitable for large occasions has been built by the management for all employees. Community halls have also been built in several areas to cater the needs of middle and lower class employees. It has allowed Tirumala Tirupati Devasthanam to construct a recreation centre and marriage hall at a vantage point for the welfare of the employees.

A computer centre has been patronized by it to encourage the employees to undergo computer training to face the development in the society.

Loans are now arranged to buy computers at a concession rate under salary deduction scheme in installments.

Perks:

Apart from the monetary benefits the management allows lot of perks to all categories.

Hospital is run by the management with qualified Doctors and Nurses and well equipped medical accessories. They have the round the clock emergency service by which free medicines and free medical treatments are given. Some serious cases are referred to leading hospitals and the entire expenses are borne by the management. An A/C ambulance for long distance travel and free checkup for children called as Baby Health Care Centre are available.

A centre for looking after young children of office going women has been established in the name "Anbalayam" or "Crèche".

Traveling is a must for employees. Hence Home Town Leave Travel Concession is given to all employees twice in a year.

For long vacation tour undertaken by the employee, the management purchases all the tickets for the entire journey (to and fro).

For motivating higher level executives, plane fare and A/c coach fares are given.

Houses are built by the management and rented for subsidiary rates and for those who do not have houses, It pays HRA as per their basic pay and the towns (A class, B class, C class types) where they are staying.

Electricity is given at a cheaper rate compared to other consumers, which is also a motivating factor to live in that Township.

Maintenance of the quarters and water charges and cleaning charges are done at concession rates as perks.

Recreation Centers for Executives and workmen are started at important locations. Community Welfare Centers, good Parks for children to play, Cine Theatre, Ayurveda Medical Care Centre, Fitness Centre, Swimming Pool, good maintained play ground in all parts of Township, environment green revolution by maintaining good number of trees for healthy air, TV station, Post office facilities, Banks in office premises etc are many of the motivation factors in the form of perks.

All provisions for a peaceful atmosphere are given to boost the morality and cheerful living, which an employee will expect.

A good Daily Market inside the Township has been created by the management for the welfare of the Public.

Well maintained roads and drainages in the Township enable the employees to lead a peaceful comfortable life and motivate their presence in the management.

Bus fares are subsidiary and cheap compared to other areas.

Free tree saplings are given to the public to improve environment.

To avoid pollution, Electro Static Precipitators have been installed as the Township is close to the Thermal Stations, where the flue gas is discharged to the atmosphere.

Above points are regarding to the living conditions.

As for the working conditions and motivation, special increments are given for talented employees and abroad training programs are arranged. Special lectures are arranged in technical side and magazine is published by the management in which the contributions and achievements of the employees and their children are published to motivate their desires.

To stimulate the leadership qualities, more powers are given to the division in charge and he is made to realize his esteemed self. Gaining confidence and to be in the good books of our boss is a vital factor for higher level executives. The respect commanded in the organization is itself a tonic for growth of the employee's future.

 All the above motivational techniques are conducive for a productivity oriented work culture. The advantages in all the factors are expected by all employees and they seek an honorable position in the society.

\

Once the living conditions are smoothened, then they can concentrate all their mind and effort in their work which will result in good production. Any distraction will affect their routine work and distract their attention. They may be forced to avail leave and attend to their mental setbacks and hence their work in the factory will be affected.

Both physically and mentally a man should be sound to put in all his efforts to enable the management to attain its objectives.

A few thousands spent by the management for motivation may result in several lakhs and crores of profits due to good work turn over in the offices and factories.

This is like throwing a small fish to catch a big fish.

A good professional manager should understand this technique positively.

View other books of Chakrapani Srinivasa

Strange India
https://www.amazon.co.uk/dp/B07S73LCTK

Kohlinoor of India: Winner Virat Kohli
https://www.amazon.co.uk/dp/B07SKNRVCT

Never Forgotten Naradar Srinivasa Rao: Most Enterprising Journalist
https://www.amazon.co.uk/dp/B07NLFY73C

How to Manage Funds in an Organization?
https://www.amazon.co.uk/dp/B00Z0Q8IF8

Wonders of Nano Technology
https://www.amazon.co.uk/dp/B07D3ZP7MC

How to become a Leader?

https://www.amazon.com/dp/B08BF4HCVX

What are the Best HRD Tactics?

https://www.amazon.co.uk/dp/B07HZ7JK18

Solar Energy Plans in Tamilnadu

https://www.amazon.co.uk/dp/B01G44ZL4K

How to Forecast Manpower Needs in an Organization: You Have The Skill!

https://www.amazon.co.uk/dp/B0111GBZKK

Infrastructure in India

https://www.amazon.co.uk/dp/B0163777RW

Accountant's Role in an Organization: A book for Accountants

https://www.amazon.co.uk/dp/B00YYHDHU0

Inland Waterways and Hydro Power in India

https://www.amazon.co.uk/dp/B015NEZMXW

Conflict Management Styles and Collective Bargaining

https://www.amazon.co.uk/dp/B00Z3B9GTW

Quiz and General Knowledge

https://www.amazon.co.uk/dp/B01N4M99S7

In Search of Paradise and Peace

https://www.amazon.co.uk/dp/B07C7F3XKM

Graphene -The God of Nano Technology

https://www.amazon.co.uk/dp/B07561LWTT

You Can Gain Power and Authority

https://www.amazon.co.uk/dp/B00YWY9QR8

HRD Systems and Management by Objectives

https://www.amazon.co.uk/dp/B016UC9UKC

International Conferences on Nanotechnology in India

https://www.amazon.co.uk/dp/B07BP8YLJZ

Holy Madhwa Saints: Get Divine Pleasure by Reading

https://www.amazon.co.uk/dp/B010WNBYU4

Trade Shows in India and Participants

https://www.amazon.co.uk/dp/B016PV1KS8

Collaboration and Intervention Techniques

https://www.amazon.co.uk/dp/B0110DLE8C

How to Plan Career and Quality Discipline in an Organization? Plan for Prosperity

https://www.amazon.co.uk/dp/B011GXOXIE

How to Speak Skillfully?
https://www.amazon.com/dp/B08BJ8PCKT

How to Supervise Efficiently?
https://www.amazon.com/dp/B08BNFYSPQ-e book